7 LBS 13 OZS

A Spiritual Journey to Motherhood

Acknowledgments

My deepest appreciation goes out to my husband Izoduwa Uwague for inspiring me through his example of persistence and dedication, for encouraging me to journal my spiritual journey to motherhood and supporting my vision to publish this book.

I would also like to recognize:

- My parents, Clive Angus and Janet Reynolds for believing in me, supporting all my endeavors and raising me with the mindset that I can achieve anything I can conceive.

- Dr. Melissa-Sue John, Tiffany Gray, Jude Somefun and Karin Wolfe for cheering me on, providing feedback and brainstorming with me during the editing process.

- Veronica Price of Picklesticks Photography for the cover photography.

- Tosan Arueyingho of JR Detos for the art design.

Special thanks to my family and friends who kept me accountable and encouraged during the entire process.

Note to Reader

Thank you for purchasing this book which supports my vision to empower and inspire women to live the best version of their life. I wrote this book to chronicle my spiritual journey through motherhood and as a reflection for my family and friends.

My decision to entitle this book with my son's birth weight, *7lbs 13 ozs* is a portrayal of how easily we can fall into the trap of weighing our worth and comparing our experiences to others. In doing so, we belittle what God has done for us.

I also found it interesting that the numbers in the scripture reference Mark 7:13 represented my son's birth weight. Mark 7:13 advises us that we nullify the Word of God because we hold on to our traditions. In other words, sometimes we get so ingrained in our culture, tradition and societal norms that we set aside spiritual wisdom.

Instead of believing what God promises us, we listen to horror stories of other people's experiences and internalize them; we lean on the internet as our sole authority and we often walk in fear. As a result, the Word of God has no effect and becomes void.

This book references the many stages mothers go through spiritually and physically because during my time of journaling my experience, the correlation of my relationship with my Heavenly Father and being a mother kept presenting itself.

After each chapter, there is a special "Thoughts" section which allows you to document your notes, questions, action items or reflection.

Contents

The Womb 1
Childbirth (Her Story) 11
Your First Love 21
The Vending Machine 27
Guard Your Gates 31
Hiccups 39
Cradle Cap 45
Cast Your Cares 53
Imagination 59
Cluster Feed 63
2 ozs 67
"Because I Said So" 73
Childproof 77
Baby Steps 83
Learning To Talk (Imitating Christ) 87
About the Author 91
My Story 93
Connect with the Author 95

The Womb

Words are creative forces releasing power and yielding positive or negative results. My husband and I used words to declare a supernatural, uncomplicated pregnancy and delivery of our child. We used our mouths as the conduit and my womb as the incubator for the care and protection of our unborn child.

The womb is a place where something originates and develops. Like a vision, the development starts in the unseen realm and as it is nurtured, it grows and matures into something that is visible.

Having a clear vision for your life is what will fuel you to accomplish your dreams and be persistent in the face of delays and adversity. Many times we become intimidated by the magnitude of the vision and, out of fear, whether it is fear of success or fear of failure, we *abort* the mission. Sometimes, we try to modify the vision God has already given us and then we become *overdue*; other times, the unknown occurs and the result is a spiritual *miscarriage*.

Whenever we receive a vision, it is critical that we cherish it. I know from experience the importance of protecting the vision because this is not the first time I became pregnant…with a vision that is…

At the age of 21, while living in New York City, I decided to buy a condominium in Florida in pursuit of the American dream. Less than one year later, I felt prompted to quit my job and I quickly dismissed the urge and carried on with my life. I enjoyed my job and I formed great friendships however the urge to leave eventually became so intense that I could not ignore the prompting anymore.

So I started a conversation with God which went something like this, "*God, I really feel you want me to leave my job but I have bills to pay!*" I truly wanted to be obedient but it didn't make *sense* to me.

Four months later, there was an inexplicable knowing that I was supposed to quit. I announced to my manager that I was resigning. She made counter offer after counter offer and I declined them all. The following week, I received an email for a job opening from a company that found my information on a job search database. I followed up on the posting, interviewed and I was accepted on the spot. I asked for time to consider the offer, I thought about it, sought for direction and declined the job offer. That didn't make *sense* either but it surely made *faith* because I knew that I was not supposed to accept that offer.

A few days later, I read my college's newsletter and saw an advertisement to teach English in China. I was always fascinated by China's culture and ability to emerge as a global giant so most of my projects focused on China. I quickly started the application and submitted step one of the process by providing the company with my name,

educational background and contact information. The second step was to prove my credentials and write a statement of purpose to explain why I wanted to join the program and convince them that I was qualified. Then I thought *"I'm not moving to China!"* Let me provide some background, I did not speak Mandarin Chinese, I butchered how to pronounce "ni hao" and I didn't know anyone in China. I closed the laptop and walked away happy that I came to my *senses*.

The same day, I received an email stating that I was accepted into the program. Based on what? My name? I was encouraged to complete the rest of the application to allow them to start processing my work visa. Again, I had that knowing that I was supposed to move to China. So I did the same thing the last time I heard God tell me to do something major. I ignored it! Maybe He will change His mind...but I knew better. I started calling my parents and mentors initiating lighthearted conversations about the possibility of moving to China. I was trying to tally the responses to see how many other people agreed that it was a crazy idea to transcend barriers based on culture, continents, language and time zones.

Being a baby in Christ, I did not know that I did not need permission from people, so instead of yielding to spiritual guidance, I sought after approval from man.

I'll save you the mystery. I decided to move to China and that's when I *conceived* and became *spiritually pregnant*. I will reiterate, it did not make *sense*, but it was *faith*.

In November, I accepted the position as a Foreign Expert to teach English beginning the following August.

For nine months, I was unemployed. During that time, God ministered to me through sermons from pastors, situations and the Holy Spirit. I learned that I was in covenant with God and He would provide all my needs. He proved himself over and over by taking care of me so I never lacked anything. I traveled to places that I wouldn't be able to go to because I wouldn't have time because I would have to work. God facilitated credit card debt cancellations; did I mention that I was unemployed? Who becomes a jetsetter and pays off credit card loans while they are unemployed? Someone who is in covenant with God! That's who!

The scripture I meditated on is found in Genesis 12: 1-3 detailing the account of God telling Abraham to leave his country, family and everything that was familiar to him to go to an unknown country and trust God to provide for him. I also meditated on Psalm 1:3 which states *"And he shall be like a tree planted by the rivers of water, that brings forth its fruit in its season, whose leaf also does not wither; and whatsoever he does will prosper."* There is an annotation by Charles Capps that *"The grace of God allows even my mistakes to prosper."* That is powerful because it comforted me that even if I was making a mistake by moving to China, God would still honor me because I was leaving in obedience to what I thought He said.

In August, I received my work visa and my plane ticket to China. I was careful not to tell everyone that I was moving to China because I knew some people would try to encourage me to *abort* the vision. Some people found out and approached me in an effort to "help me" see that I was making a mistake. My response was "*I truly believe that I am supposed to go, I already signed my contract and I have to honor that. If you think I made a mistake, then pray for me that the grace and mercy of God will be on my life and allow me to accomplish the purpose.*"

Whenever someone conceives a vision, a dream or an idea, like a fetus in a mother's womb, it has to be protected. We would not give our babies to someone we don't trust or know, so why would should we be so negligent by telling our vision to the wrong person? At this point, God had prepared me and I was so established in my identity as a fearless and victorious woman of God who could do all things with His help.

As a part of my contract, the Chinese host school provided housing accommodations for me. There was an American woman who lived in the apartment prior to my arrival. Her contract just ended so she moved back to America. When I arrived at what would be my new apartment, I noticed a few pictures and small articles that she left behind in my new home. I went to the bathroom to freshen up to prepare for an introductory dinner with the Chinese school administration. I saw a frame and smiled in amazement as I read the words, "*And he shall be like a tree planted by the rivers of water, that brings forth its fruit in its season, whose leaf also does not wither; and whatsoever he does will prosper.*" That was the same scripture from Psalm 1:3 that I was meditating on! If that's not confirmation, then what is?

My original teaching contract was for ten months but I had such an amazing and fulfilling time that I renewed my contract and stayed for two years. The Chinese Foreign Policy Affairs offered me a five year contract and the only reason I declined is because I knew if I stayed any longer, there would be little chance or desire to move back to New York and I wanted to return to my family.

What I realized in hindsight is that the job offer I received after quitting my beloved job in New York was a distraction to prevent me from fulfilling my real purpose.

While I was in China, I started an empowerment program for some of my students who had body image and self-esteem issues and I mentored hundreds of women. My purpose was to make a positive impact in the lives of everyone I encountered through academic teaching, counseling and inspiration.

My nine months of unemployment were a time of preparation, character development and reassurance that God can be trusted. China was my *baby* and having fully conceived, I gave birth to the vision God had in store for me. That was my *spiritual pregnancy*.

Three years after I returned to New York, I was pursued by a gorgeous man whose character and integrity preceded him. We met five years prior and within nine quick months, we courted, I accepted his engagement proposal and we exchanged marriage vows. A few months after we got married, I learned that I was pregnant, in the natural realm this time. I believed Jeremiah 29:11 that the plans God has towards me are good and they are not to harm me.

Some people may not understand the magnitude of bringing a child into the world. It is not to be taken lightly because it is a God given assignment so I sometimes call myself one of God's babysitters. We really could be rearing the next president, political leader, spiritual teacher, inventor, engineer, or artist.

While our child was in the womb, my husband wrote out some affirmations to speak over our child and asked me to confess them daily. The affirmations were powerful assertions about our child's character, intellect and integrity. Most of them were derived from the Bible and I told my unborn child *"You are strong in the Lord and in the power of His might, you have character, you do what is right because it's right"*. Even after his birth, we are still releasing these powerful statements over him. Whenever someone notices something that we confessed and envisioned about our son, we are not surprised because we know that Job 22:28 states that *"When we speak and decree a thing, we are establishing things on the earth!"*

It is important to speak affirmations over your child because if you don't define who they are, someone else will! What does God say about your child?

As a child of God, He calls us heirs and overcomers. He says that we are *more* than conquerors. Your child is an answer and was created to solve a specific problem.

Jeremiah 1:5 says *"Before I formed you in the womb I knew you, before you were born I set you apart; I appointed you as a prophet to the nations"*. God knows our unborn children and absolutely has a purpose for them to accomplish.

There may be tests and attacks on your physical and spiritual vision and it can be stolen by self-defeating thoughts and negative words or opposition from someone who does not support the vision. So regardless of the circumstances concerning your pregnancy, God can take that test and turn it into a testimony.

So women, as you exercise your superpower of growing a human, be gentle to yourself and do not make comparisons with others because in doing so, you belittle what God has given you.

Thoughts

Childbirth (Her Story)

In Genesis 3: 16 in the account of Adam and Eve, Eve received a curse of severe pains in childbearing and painful labor to give birth to children. The good news is that when Jesus agreed to die for our sins, Galatians 3:13 tells us that He took on the burden and redeemed us from the curse. 1 Timothy 2:15 reassures us that by continuing in faith, love and holiness with self-control, women will be spared in childbirth. When I read that these scriptures said I would be redeemed from the curse of childbirth, I took that to heart and believed that I could have an uncomplicated pregnancy and delivery because I know that having a child is a blessing.

From my observation, it seems as if people who have never had babies are more afraid of childbirth than those who have actually experienced it. Is it the fear of the unknown? Is it from the horror stories or is it because they were told about the curse relating to childbirth?
Research shows that feelings of dread, fear and anxiety produce certain signals which tell your mind to fight or flee. If you train your mind to latch on to stressful outcomes and you worry about the future, your mind will allow your body to become tense and cause complications. The stress and tension your body experiences the hours leading up to your delivery can make it much worse than it would have been if these stressful thoughts were replaced with positive ones.

There are huge psychosomatic connections between mind and body illnesses so if you already envision the pain, your body just manifests what you created. Whenever someone wanted to tell me their horror stories of childbirth, trauma and sleepless nights; I respectfully ended the conversation.

Words and thoughts are more powerful than we may realize, and we have to ensure that we are not making negative affirmations about childbirth. I know people who have said continually, maybe jokingly, that they know they will have a lengthy tormenting labor and when it IS horrible, they exclaim "I knew it would be this way". Well what if this worked in the reverse, if you declared how uncomplicated or supernatural it would be and then it was?

If you experienced complications in your pregnancy or delivery, then I sympathize with you and I want you to know that I am not judging you. You should not feel condemned and I am not saying that your experience was your own fault or a lack of trust in God. I just never understood why I had to suffer because I wanted to bring a baby into this world.

As a result, I conditioned my mind that I would not have a horrific experience during my delivery. I am aware that morning sickness, nausea and painful births are common and I again want to reiterate that I am very sensitive to women who have suffered.

My heart goes out to these women, not only because of the physical pain but the emotional trauma or stress that may accompany the experience.

I'll share my story...

I truly enjoyed being pregnant, maybe it is my personality because I love new experiences or because I know a baby is a gift from God and I personally know and heard of far too many women who wanted to conceive but could not have children. With that knowledge and an attitude of gratitude, I couldn't take this gift for granted. I documented my pregnancy by taking pictures and keeping a calendar. I honored my bump and I looked forward to the big gush where I would exclaim "my water broke" and get excited about delivering a baby.

My due date was Sunday August 31, 2014, and on Friday August 29th, I went to work, stopped by a restaurant for a going away party and then went home to seek refuge from the hot sunny day.

I cut into a huge watermelon and popped piece after piece in my mouth to try to cool down. I had a busy weekend planned so I knew I needed to get some rest.

The following day, my church would be hosting a Back to School event in a park to giveaway school supplies to children in the community. After the event, I planned to attend our weekly church service.

I proceeded to lie down and I felt an intense urge to urinate. I didn't get to the bathroom in time but I released what hadn't already come down. I woke up several times during the night because I felt a lot of moisture *down there* and my underwear was damp. I made it through the night and managed to get a good night's sleep.

I showed up at the Back to School event ready to serve the children. A few minutes later, I went to the bathroom because I continued to feel the excess moisture I had felt the night before. I thought *"It must be really hot out here why I am sweating so much or maybe I just ate too much watermelon last night!"*

Eventually the damp feeling became uncomfortable so I decided to call my doctor. She asked a few questions and then I confirmed that I was not having any contractions. She said that if I was concerned enough to call, I should probably go to the hospital. I thanked her, ended the call and walked back over to the event.

About three hours later, I decided to take her advice and go to the hospital. I ate one of my favorite meals, Jamaican stew peas and rice, knowing that if I got admitted that would probably be my last meal until I delivered the baby.

I thought to myself *"Oh that's what everyone kept talking about when they said they would leak if they sneezed, laughed or coughed."*

I called my husband and told him that I was feeling fine but I just wanted to get a checkup so he didn't need to come. I packed a small bag and proceeded to the train station.

As I exited my apartment, my husband was approaching and he also realized that I was not in any pain. He still advised however that I should at least take a cab since I didn't need him to come with me.

I hopped in a taxi and after observing the gorgeous water views of the Henry Hudson Parkway; I arrived at Mount Sinai St. Luke's-Roosevelt Hospital.

I explained that I am not sure if I am leaking because there is pressure on my bladder so I wanted to be checked. The triage service, professionalism and efficiency of the hospital were very impressive.

After a few minutes of waiting, I was given a bed and a resident doctor confirmed that the "moisture" I was feeling was leakage because my water broke that Friday night! I was expecting the big Hollywood gush so when that trickle happened, I figured I probably just really needed to empty a full bladder or that there was pressure from the weight of the baby already descending!

The caveat was that even though my water broke and I was leaking amniotic fluid, I was only 2.5 cm dilated and I had to be fully dilated at 10 cm.

It had been more than 24 hours since my water broke so to prevent an infection and for the safety of the baby, the doctors decided to admit me. I sent a text to my husband and friend, and they came to the hospital and by 10pm, I was in what would be my delivery room.

I really wanted the entire process to happen naturally but I understood the risks involved so when offered Pitocin to induce my labor, I accepted. Pitocin is a brand of a synthetic form of the drug oxytocin, which encourages or fortifies contractions to speed up childbirth.

We set the atmosphere with music and waited for a miracle. During my labor, my nurse checked on me periodically saying, "Why are you still smiling? I need to hear some screaming".

She was very personable and at one point I told her a story about when I visited her home country. She was smiling as I recounted my memorable visit to Russia and then her facial expression changed and she exclaimed *"Did you feel that?"* I responded, *"No, what?"* She pointed to the chart and said *"that"*; she showed me a huge spike in my contractions and she was amazed that I was not in distress.

I was having a pain free labor and experiencing contractions without feeling them!

There was an influx of questions from nurses and doctors about why I was not feeling pain, I shifted my focus from the promises I meditated on and thought, *"Can I really have a pain free delivery?"* For the next five hours, I did not feel any contractions but at 3am, I felt about five sharp contractions as I shifted my focus to my body and the ability to truly have a pain free labor.

Once the doctors realized that I had a contraction, they were relieved and actually seemed happy but they were still amazed at how uncomplicated the process was. By 4am, I was finally 10 cm dilated and the doctor advised that even though I was fully dilated, I probably wouldn't have a baby until the next two hours.

I begged her to just check once more before she left. She turned back to me and looked at me in disbelief and said *"Rose-Anne, can you try **not** to push?"* The doctor explained that my son's head was *crowning* and already visible.

All the doctors and nurses started putting on their gloves and gearing up so that we could do some practice rounds of breathing and pushing. I pushed four times and the resident doctor said, *"OK just one more time"*. I looked at her thinking *"Yea, I have seen the movies, I know one more time does not mean one more time."* I pushed one more time and at 4:16 am, the doctor threw a screaming baby on my chest. Everything happened so fast that for a split second I thought, *"Now, what is that and where did it come from?"*

The doctors started calling me "*rock star*" and "*superstar*". They had the "super" part right, but what that really was… was supernatural.

I rejected the idea that the birth of a baby had to be horrifying and God added His super to my natural and in sixteen uncomplicated minutes, a new human was born into this world.

The hospital and the doctors are very big on immediate skin to skin contact so they did not clean off the baby before throwing him on my chest.

He opened his mouth and showed off the power of his lungs and he screamed profusely. I rocked him as I looked up to catch a glimpse of my husband's face. I comforted our baby saying "*It's OK; it's OK*". I'm not sure if it was because he heard my voice or if his performance was over but he calmed down, looked up at me, smacked his lips two times, shifted into position and latched on for his first meal!

That's my story and the rest is *herstory*!

Thoughts

Your First Love

Revelations 2: 3-4 "You have persevered and have endured hardships for My name, and have not grown weary. Yet I hold this against you: *"You have forsaken the love you had at first."*

I asked my friend, Tiffany, to explain what she thought the scripture meant and she gleaned that sometimes we get so caught up in doing things for God, that we forget...*God*. Sometimes we do so much in ministry or mission work FOR God that we neglect the One we are doing it for. The snippet of the scripture *"You have forsaken the love you had at first"* stuck out to me because sometimes the beginning of our Christian relationship has so much passion, zeal and enthusiasm and then we get so absorbed in life that we forget the depth of the love we had for God.

There are two points that I want to convey. The first is to remind you not to be so enthralled in the joys of motherhood that you don't have time to spend with your Heavenly Father. One of my favorite ministers, Carol Jones said something very simple and profound, "If you are too busy to spend time with God, you are too busy!"

The second point is to be cautious that you don't become so wrapped up in the unrealistic attainment of being a perfect mother or the mundane routines of motherhood that you lose sight of the joys of motherhood.

As Christians, we sometimes devote our lives to God and spend countless hours praising Him, reading our Bibles, and we become eager to learn more about Him. We appreciate Him and rave about everything God does for us from the parking spot in front of the mall to the answered prayer about receiving a promotion. Sadly, for some of us that fire is quenched, the passion dies down and worshiping God becomes mundane. Spending time with God becomes an action item like something to do out of obligation or fear based on bad teaching that if you don't worship Him then *"God's going to get you"*.

Before moving to China, my husband and I served in the Children's Ministry at my church. I thoroughly enjoyed serving there and anticipated spending time with the children. I also assisted with the administrative tasks including tracking attendance, creating schedules and meeting agendas. I ensured that the weekly reports were sent to the church office on time, I typed up minutes and maintained a binder with updated information. I worked on lesson plans, I taught classes and I interviewed prospective members. I arrived early to serve and left late. I was so engrossed in doing the *work of God* and all my activities *for Him* that I sometimes forsook my personal time *with Him*.

I noticed the analogy between Christian life and motherhood. We start off with the same zeal when we have our babies. If you've ever listened in or participated in a conversation with a new mother, you will hear exclamations like:

Guess what happened today?
My little one smiled at me.
Oh he burped, how cute!
He said "dada".
She crawled
He walked
Another diaper change! His digestive system is so perfect!
(Ok fine, maybe no one says that but you get the point.)

The list goes on and on about how precious our children are to us. We praise our child for everything they do because everything our babies do is *precious* or *adorable* or *perfect*. Even their crying is…*precious*…

It always amazes me how quickly what we did for the sheer joy of doing becomes the very essence of what becomes overwhelming. Activities like feeding the baby, making bottles, changing diapers could easily prevent me from spending time with God if I didn't prioritize and keep things in the proper order to remember my first love.

It's a balancing act to ensure that we don't get too wrapped up in loving our children that we minimize our time with God and that we don't get bogged down by tending to our children that we no longer enjoy motherhood. Now that we have tackled the issue, do not allow condemnation to creep in, just get back on track. Here are some practical steps on how to make the necessary changes:

- God loves spending time with you so do not make spending time with God a law or an obligation. We wouldn't want someone to spend time with us because they felt it was mandatory so let's prioritize fellowshipping with God by making time to cultivate a relationship, feed yourself spiritually and getting to know Him by reading the Bible, praying, praising and offering thanksgiving.

- Ask God for help to reignite your zeal just as David prayed in Psalm 51:12 "Restore unto me the joy of thy salvation." Regardless of the reason you lost your zeal, that passion can be reignited! When you are hungry, do you dwell on the fact that you waited too long to eat or do you just go get something to eat. You just eat, right?

Return to your first love and make first things first!

Thoughts

The Vending Machine

Matthew 6:33 says *"Seek first the Kingdom of God and His righteousness, and all these things will be given to you as well."*

Have you ever felt that your relationships are one-sided? As if you are the only one giving in the relationship? Maybe that you are being taken advantage of? Ever felt that the other person is only in the relationship for what they can get from you?

My friend Katie asked me to identify the most challenging factor of motherhood. After careful consideration, I explained that I was really enjoying motherhood but the task that I least enjoyed was pumping breast milk! I found it to be a very daunting task. She continued, "The reason I asked is because my friend has a newborn and she feels like she spends her entire day feeding her son." Her friend complained that the baby did not have any personality and she didn't feel as if she had a relationship with him, she just felt that she was there to fill his demands with nothing in return.

What she was explaining is that in return for her hours of changing diapers, breastfeeding, giving baths and soothing the baby to sleep, all she wanted was a smile or a few minutes of play time with her beloved baby. Instead, all she received was *me, me, me – feed me, change me, bathe me, soothe me…*

While I didn't share that sentiment concerning my son, I immediately thought about my personal relationship with God. Was I using God as my personal genie or vending machine? Insert five minutes of prayer in exchange for a new job!

"God I could really use a new house. It would be great if I had a new car; I could really use some more peace, can you work on that God?"

God I need that…

God I want that…

God, can I have that?

In 2 Corinthians 9:8, we learn that *"God is able to make all grace abound toward us."* So instead of being overly focused on what He can give you, focus on strengthening your relationship with Him.

Matthew 6:33 encourages us to seek God's face and not just His hands. The interesting twist, however, is that while God wants an intimate relationship with you, Philippians 4:19 tells us that He is also eager to fill all our demands and He wants to give us those desires of our hearts!

Relationships are nurtured by spending time together and getting to know and trust each other. If every time I go to God with a list of demands of what I want and what I need, then I really don't have a relationship with Him. I am simply an opportunist trying to get favors from Him. *How is your relationship with God?*

Whenever I start off my morning with worries instead of thankfulness, I am reminded of a comment from Joyce Meyer. In what was supposed to be her *prayer time*, she started complaining about all that was going wrong. Eventually, she felt convicted and had to answer the question, *"Are you here to fellowship with Me {God} or your problems?"*

This had a tremendous effect on me because I realized that sometimes I do the same thing! I was using my prayer time to talk about everything that was going wrong instead of thanking God for everything that was going right. Thanksgiving Day should not just be an annual event; we should strive to live a life of gratitude for all that God has already done for us.

Thoughts

Guard Your Gates

"See to it that no one carries you off as spoil or makes you yourselves captive by his so-called philosophy and intellectualism and vain deceit (idle fancies and plain nonsense), following human tradition (men's ideas of the material rather than the spiritual world", just crude notions following the rudimentary and elemental teachings of the universe and disregarding {the teachings of} Christ (the Messiah)." Colossians 2:8 The Message Bible

The Bible talks about the importance of guarding your ears, your heart and your mind and putting on protective gear. We have so much access to information through social media, the news, friends, family and even strangers. If you don't know the Word of God, how will you know what is contrary to the Word of God? How will you be able to effectively guard your gates if you don't know what should be denied access?

Why is it important to guard your heart? Your heart is the breeding ground for things to happen in your life so you can't give everyone access to it. There are so many ways that your heart can become affected through your physical senses, especially through what you hear and what you see; but it's our responsibility to keep our hearts protected.

Be careful who you listen to because words are seeds that are planted in your heart, and it grows and germinates in your thought life.

A seed is planted by sprinkling it on the ground then covering it with soil, so are thoughts planted in our hearts. Well-meaning comments may germinate in our hearts and thought life and produce corruptible seed. We have to be intentional and purposeful in our decisions to share or accept information.

Who are we spending time with? Do these people uplift us? Do we feel refreshed and energized after speaking to them or discouraged and defeated? In essence, *who has access to our hearts?*

Two days after being discharged from the hospital with my *precious* newborn, I found myself in a state of interrogation. I was bombarded with questions from family, friends, doctors and strangers.

Will you breastfeed exclusively?
When will you introduce formula?
Are you going to pump breast milk when you go back to work? For how long?

Most people had good reasons for asking the questions and their intentions were pure. Some wanted to offer advice, share stories or simply reminisce about their own experience. Prior to being questioned about my plans, I was confident that everything would work out.

When I was pregnant, I learned the importance of guarding my heart and not allowing fear to enter and contaminate my faith.

I remember one woman telling me about how much milk she produced. She had such a surplus that she would get help from her husband to help her switch out the bottles as her flow was so heavy! I got excited thinking that would happen to me as well. Everything was going well. I was breastfeeding my son, he was happy and healthy and I was rested and content.

Then he started to take longer naps and the milk started to harden and it was very painful. I already knew that I needed to pump to prevent any buildup of excess milk and prevent the pain associated with it.

The baby isn't getting enough milk; you have to give him formula
You aren't producing enough milk...
Eat more.
Pump more.
Nurse more.

Again, what was the motive? To help me, but excessive advice can be overwhelming!

What was the outcome? Fear and emotional exhaustion!

Then I thought, *"Maybe I can't produce enough to sustain my son. Maybe I won't be able to build up a surplus before I returned to work."*

The first few times I pumped, I expressed teaspoons. It was humiliating. I made the mistake of mentioning it to a few seasoned mothers to get advice and support; instead,

I became discouraged and anxious. Do you see the progression of how I went from a confident woman who would have so much milk I could feed a village to wondering if I would be able to sustain my own son?

FEAR is an acronym for False Evidence Appearing Real. While I was in the midst of the situation, I was afraid that I would not be able to produce enough milk; but when I returned to work, I was able to express enough for each day so I was actually one day ahead of him. By the following week, I was coming home with an extra bottle per day!

Trust God regardless of how situations look. While it would have been nice to be a few more days ahead of him, I had to focus on one day at a time.

A few weeks after my son was born, a friend came to visit me. As he held my son impressed by how alert he was, my son broke his gaze and turned to look at me as I was approaching them. My witty friend commented "Don't think he is looking at you because you are his mother, all he sees is a giant feeding bottle." I started laughing with the thought that it was partially true!

Two weeks later, I went to visit a friend who just gave birth to her second child. In a short three hour period, my son initiated feeding two times. He normally ate every two to three hours but I didn't give it much thought.

My friend remarked that I needed to learn how to decipher when he is feeding for nutritional purposes versus for comfort. She continued, *"Ro, I think he is using you as a pacifier."* Maybe he was and one could argue, *"Well, what's wrong with that?"* Would he be able unable to calm himself or go to sleep on his own because he relied on me to do it? Was she trying to insinuate that my child would have dependency issues and not be able to cope? No, she was not saying that at all, but based on that suggestion, I allowed fear to creep in that I wouldn't know the difference between him wanting to feed for nourishment rather than comfort.

For the next few days, every time my son gave me hunger cues, the thought arose, *"Are you using me as a pacifier or are you really hungry? Do you just see me as a giant feeding bottle?"* While the intentions of my friends were pure, their words penetrated my thinking. See how subtly our hearts and minds can be invaded? Notice that I didn't have a problem with the frequency of my son feeding and I didn't think it was unusual or too frequent until it was *suggested*. Why did I start second guessing? Could this have been a negative inroad into my thinking?

How are thoughts created? By words, pictures and images that we are exposed to. Let's take for an example that you see an image of a gorgeous home. Maybe you saw it in a magazine, a TV program or a social media profile.

If you start to experience discontentment about the size of your home, then a seed was planted into your heart based on what entered your "eye gate".

If someone shares a romantic story of something that was done for them and you feel inferior in your own relationship or because you don't have that kind of relationship, then a seed was planted based on what entered your "ear gate".

Proverbs 4:23 advises us to watch over our hearts with all diligence because out of it flows the issues of life. Our heart is the center of our life, and if it is unhealthy, it will impact everything else.

The first step in guarding our hearts is to realize and accept that it is our personal responsibility and we must remain accountable because we don't know when it will get wounded. The second step is to filter information we receive. We don't have to accept every piece of advice we receive.

Everyone has opinions, but not all are useful. Use discernment and be vigilant in deciding whose advice you internalize and by doing so you will guard your gates!

Thoughts

Hiccups

The issue with hiccups is that you cannot predict when they will come. They are annoying and irritating. They are a minor inconvenience and you don't know when they will go away. We know that having a hiccup is not a grave issue but when we experience minor delays or hiccups in our lives, we sometimes overreact or worry unnecessarily.

I will not debate about what causes hiccups because I have read numerous articles about the cause and all are far more frightening than the actual hiccups! I watched my son as those annoying hiccups started, as he gasped after each contraction, he just looked at me and laughed. Even though he seemed unaffected by it and I knew that they would subside very quickly, I felt helpless as I watched him. He did not cry or get frustrated, he just continued on with life.

I am not insinuating that my son trained himself on how to react to a hiccup; his decision to laugh it off was based on his personality and my reaction to show him that it was not a big deal.

Maybe if we train ourselves to have more positive responses to negative circumstances, we would enjoy more peaceful lives.

When I started the outline of this book, it flowed so seamlessly but when it came to actually drafting the book, there were so many hiccups, roadblocks and challenges. Some of the hiccups included the fact that I lost some of the content because my iPad stopped working and the only resolution Apple could offer was for me to reset and delete all the content or purchase a new iPad; my laptop stopped working and I lost some of the content again, my personal life got busier and I became uninspired. I also wasted a lot of time during the editing process because I was relying on other people's approval instead of trusting God to be my main source of wisdom.

I'm not saying that you will have hiccups in life because I will not make negative declarations over your life. Furthermore, I don't want you to believe that a life of hiccups is the norm. What I do want to communicate is that how we view situations and what we speak about them largely affects the outcome. Our perspective on the situation largely determines our reactions to the issue. I wish I would laugh at the minor hiccups in my life the way my son reacted to his.

When I was pregnant, I was so inundated with positive confessions about how my pregnancy would be that it became natural to speak positively over my pregnancy. I have noticed that whenever I say something negative, it turns out that way and of course I declare, "I knew that would happen." Well I should expect that because I set it in motion with the power of my tongue.

When we respond positively to a test or trial we are facing, instead of throwing a temper tantrum, we are expressing our confidence in the Word of God. John 16:33 says, *"I have said these things to you, that in Me {God} you may have peace. In the world you will have tribulation. But take heart; I have overcome the world."* So while I felt helpless watching my son go through his hiccup, I know that we serve a mighty God who is able to help us through a *hiccup* if we encounter one and He encourages us to be courageous because Jesus has overcome the world.

James 1:2-4: *Consider it pure **joy** when we face trials and testing of our faith because being tested produces endurance and patience so that we can be mature and perfect wanting nothing.*

How can we respond positively to something that is negative? Well, it depends on what you know.

If you know that you always win in the end, then you will have joy as you remain patient. You may ask, so how do we handle trials? How do we practically apply this to our lives?

1. *Perspective* - Change your mindset – *Rejoice*
   Why in the world would I rejoice when I face temptations, trials or tests? We don't rejoice because we are *in* a situation, we rejoice because we know we are coming *through* victoriously!

Think about a wrestling match that has been staged; the person who knows that they are declared the winner will not be concerned about the clothesline, elbow drop or DDT because they already know the outcome. Joy comes from what you know. If you know that you are a conqueror, your perspective on trials will change because you consider it a fixed fight, and you know you already won!

2. *Be patient* – Do not allow hiccups to steal your joy, use it as an opportunity to develop and mature. The Message Bible states that when we are under pressure, we show our true character! When patience has completed her perfect work, we will not want or lack anything. So don't try to get out of anything prematurely!

Believe that you will not be plagued by the hiccups of life but be prepared to overcome any challenge that may come your way.

Thoughts

Cradle Cap

Cradle cap (otherwise known as infantile seborrheic dermatitis) is an annoying scalp issue that affects adults and babies alike. It is an inflammatory skin condition that looks like a bad case of dandruff. Not all babies will be affected by cradle cap and doctors still don't know why some babies experience it. Researchers of cradle cap explored that it is not a matter of hygiene but there is still no concrete reason for why it develops.

When my son was six weeks old, I started to notice white flakes in between his full head of curly hair. I applied coconut oil and gently used a brush to get rid of the intruder. Then the next day, I noticed that it was in a different spot! I became obsessed with it and I peered in between every little curl to make sure that I got rid of all the scales. Why is this happening? I did everything I thought I was supposed to do. I washed his hair, I kept it moisturized. I thought I did everything right so needless to say, this development made me feel guilty and anxious.

There is a possibility that your baby will develop cradle cap, and if it happens, please do not think it is something you did or did not do, please do not blame yourself or think it is your fault. Whenever something happens to our children, we are quick to blame ourselves or feel as if were negligent or there was a lax on good parenting.

If the scalp is dry, it may create minimal itching; otherwise the baby is totally unaffected. It usually bothers the parents more than the child because of its unsightly appearance. It is very harmless and it is not painful.

The cradle cap soon became a distant memory because the issue eventually resolved itself in its own time. I thought that by scratching out the scales and working at it faster, I would expedite the process.

Are there other minor things in life that you become fixated on or spend your time scratching against the surface? I remember when I was looking for an apartment a few years ago. I had just moved back from China and I knew what I wanted and I made it a joint effort with God. I prayed for direction and guidance. I asked God for supernatural grace and favor and did my part in the natural by researching different websites and contacting realtors.

Then, I become obsessed with finding a new home and giving God deadlines like "*OK God, I need a place by December 29th*". Then after the time would pass, I would remind Him that I needed a place and offer a new deadline saying, "*So maybe there was some miscommunication Lord, I need this apartment by January 15th, please, and thank you. Amen*!"

At the time I was living with a friend and while she was in no hurry to get rid of me, I just had these self-inflicted deadlines that I needed to adhere to. My family and friends did not receive phone calls or text messages from me because I spent my lunch breaks and free time surfing real estate rental websites, contacting realtors and visiting apartments. My phone contact list was filled with numbers from landlords, real estate professionals and addresses of potential new homes.

Eventually, I removed God from the equation and I changed from being in a place of rest cooperating with God to a place of toiling because I was afraid that I would not get the apartment, not necessarily when I needed it but when I wanted it.

It was similar to how I spent my time getting rid of the cradle cap. I brushed out the scales before I gave my son a bath, I washed his hair while I gave him a bath, I brushed them out after I gave him a bath. I checked on the progress while he was sleeping and every time I remembered about them. The intention was to be a good mother, monitor it and keep it under control, but the mindset was one of fear that it would worsen.

There is a huge difference between being diligent and being obsessive. The difference is your motive and your mindset. When you are trying to receive something, you pray about it, set out with your ambitions and diligently work to receive the promises of God.

You know that it is just a matter of time before you receive the manifestation of it. When you are working tirelessly, not sleeping because you are up trying to make something happen, you have crowned yourself God, engaging in self-effort and you are working out of fear.
Fear of the unknown. Fear that what God promised won't come to pass. Fear that you won't get what you need when you need it. Fear that you are stuck!

I found an apartment and it came off the market before I decided to apply for it. I declared that it would come back on the market and it did! (I was actually surprised when I saw the posting again but God was reminding me about the power of my words.) When I went back to the area the apartment was located, I decided to ask around about the neighborhood. I spoke to a woman who worked at a facility next door to the apartment building and she said *"Baby, do yourself a favor and don't even consider moving in that building! There ain't nothing but drug addicts and ex-convicts in that building."* God protected me from receiving a counterfeit!

So I am sure you want to know what happened with the apartment. On February 2nd, about six weeks after I started looking for my new home, I found the apartment that I wanted! I found it online; I contacted the broker and went to visit it.

There was a couple waiting to see the apartment as well and I figured they would take it right away because they had a baby and the apartment offered a junior bedroom that would be perfect for a nursery or an office. I asked them if they were interested but they were still deciding and said they wanted to see other options. The apartment was exactly what I wrote down in my vision book, except for the fact that it was more than my budget allowed for.

The broker asked me what I thought about the place and considering I recently returned from China, I had the mindset that "everything is negotiable, right?" I told her that I was interested but it was more than I could afford. I moved into that apartment paying $100 less than the low end of my price range! The broker and the landlord both went down on the rent and the landlord paid the broker fee! Now that's supernatural grace and favor!

I had no idea on January 29th that I was only four days away from my new home. I stressed on January 30th and toiled on February 1st not knowing that I was hours away from my answered prayer.

I did not find my perfect apartment by toiling and losing sleep over it, the apartment was not on the market the previous days when I was being preoccupied with finding it. To add balance, clearly you cannot sit around expecting the apartment to magically appear, but you should not lose your peace because you are trying to make something happen that you don't have full control over.

So the next time you have a situation, consider the following:

1. Don't allow condemnation to creep in or take blame for something that happens to you or your child, especially when you did not know how to prevent it.

2. Don't try to use confessions or positive declarations like a magic trick or become overly obsessed with your situation.

3. Do not be anxious for anything but in all things, trust God!

Thoughts

Cast Your Cares

"Give all your worries and cares to God, for He cares about you."
1 Peter 5:7

Have you ever felt like there aren't enough hours in the day? You wake up, get dressed, leave home, arrive at your destination, return home, eat dinner and before you know it, it's time for bed so that you can get up and do it all over again. My personal daily woes went something like this:

I need to pump!

I haven't eaten breakfast and it is 2PM!

I have to cook!

I still haven't done the laundry

I have to go out today but my clothes don't fit, what am I going to wear?

Don't you feel tired just reading this? Your thoughts alone can make you feel exhausted!

In addition to my very busy life and adjusting to motherhood, I was having difficulty expressing breast milk.

It wasn't that I wasn't producing enough; I just didn't know how to get it out! You would think that a $500 pump would do the job but it didn't. Pumping was the bane of my existence!

I created an ideal in my head that I was going to have surplus of milk so that when I returned to work, my son would have more than enough for one month! In retrospect, I wasted so much time being preoccupied with it.

While I didn't have the weeks of supply that I anticipated, I was always at least a day ahead for his supply, and he was never hungry. I mean honestly, if I realized that I could not pump enough in advance, there is such a thing as formula, right?

Matthew 6:31 warns us not to think about tomorrow because today carries its own worries! I was stressing about what my newborn would drink but my son never worried about whether I would have enough milk for him, he just trusted that he would be fed and he was fed.

I've noticed that children aren't usually concerned about provision. They make their demands and expect for them to be filled. As Christians, we should strive to obtain that childlike faith.

Sometimes when we think that we won't have provision, we should think back to all the times that God showed up and showed out in the nick of time. We need to have a flashback and think about all the times we thought we weren't going to make it but actually came out pretty well.

While it can be beneficial to be proactive and you may take comfort in knowing that everything is planned out, you have to realize that sometimes plans are a false sense of security because there are external factors that cannot be controlled and quite simply things change. It is better to create a map of a desired outcome and be flexible and content even if it does not work out that way. Do not use the excuse *"I'm a planner"* to become anxious or overly obsessed with the future.

Finally, you may be tempted to feel overwhelmed by how much you have to juggle but be encouraged by 1 Peter 5:7 knowing that God cares for you and you can hand over your worries to Him.

A stranger asked me about my baby's sleeping habits and I told her that he slept very well. She shared her own story that her daughter used to cry from 11pm to 5am. Every time the baby cried, she would give her a bottle of formula not realizing that what was being fed was contributing to the discomfort. She learned by trial and error what she needed to eliminate.

After listening to so many stories about how people spoil babies, I developed a fear that if I cuddled my baby too much, he would be spoiled. While taking a long shower, I heard my baby crying so I prepared to go to him but within a few minutes he fell asleep!

Another time I tried to teach my baby independence and how to fall asleep on his own. He whined for a few minutes but then he started to cry profusely and it turned into the hunger cry which I can now differentiate from the "pick me up" cry. I felt so guilty because my baby wasn't crying because he wanted to be held, he was crying because he was hungry.

Why did I listen to people who caused me to carry the care instead of casting it? I needed to do what was best for my son because what works for your child may not necessarily work for mine and vice versa.

The good thing is that babies are very resilient and forgiving and there are many different ways to achieve similar results, so just make a mental note of what works and what doesn't.

Cast your cares on God because He cares for you.

Thoughts

Imagination

As I was researching activities to do with my son, I came across a playground that facilitates and encourages the use of imagination in children. Instead of traditional playgrounds that have swings, slides and permanent fixtures; loose pieces are placed all around the playground that allow children to creatively maneuver and create scenes as they desire.

I thought that the playground was very interesting because encouraging the use of imagination can be a huge cultural difference. Some parents encourage the use of imagination while others shun it by reprimanding children to refrain from talking to imaginary friends fearing that the child has gone mad.

There is an old wives' tale that children smile at the ceiling because they can see the spiritual realm. Sometimes I see my son looking at the ceiling and smiling. He will stare intently as if his imagination is running rampant so I ask him jestingly, "*Are you looking at angels?*" I purposed in my heart to support the use of my son's imagination so if he decides to play the imaginary trombone, I sing along to his tune. If he takes his toy cellphone and places it to his ear, I am quick to say "hello" and pretend to be the other person on the line.

There is a story in the Bible about the Tower of Babel. A group of people who spoke the same language shared the same vision of building a tower that would reach Heaven. In this account, we learn that when people act in unison, they can do anything they desire to do. Genesis 11:6 states *"Nothing they imagined to do could be withheld from them."* Simply put, if you can envision a thing, it can be achieved. Conception takes place in the realm of the imagination.

A few years ago, I created a vision board for some things I wanted at that particular time. I imagined myself getting a new job that I would love, being debt-free and meeting a man I wanted to marry. Eventually, I had to take down the vision board because everything on that board became a reality!

It happened again with the brownstone in Brooklyn after I finally stopped toiling, did research and started visualizing. I wrote in my journal that I wanted to live in a large one bedroom apartment on a tree-lined street with large windows, great sunlight and ample space. I received all that and more. My brownstone had 1 ½ bedrooms with a large living room; access to the rooftop with the view of the New York City skyline and the Empire State Building. It also gave access to a gorgeous park and it was walking distance from three different subway stations.

Like an architect with an imagination and a blueprint, I received exactly what I envisioned!

How will you use your imagination today?

We can learn a lot by observing children's behavior and their response to situations. The practice of engaging imagination is widely used in religion, sales training and empowerment courses. It is often called visualizations or meditation.

What if we used our imagination positively as much as we used it negatively in the form of worry and anxiety? That's all worry is! Negative meditation.

Will you *see* yourself as victorious based on Romans 8:37, which reminds us that, *"Yet in all these things we are more than conquerors through Him who loved us."*

Will you *see* yourself as healed based on God's promise in Isaiah 53:5, which states, *"But He {Jesus} was wounded for our transgressions, He was bruised for our iniquities: the chastisement of our peace was upon him; and with His stripes we are healed."*

What would you be doing if you did not feel sick? What would you do if you believed that you were healed? Would you sit up in the bed all day or would you be out pursuing your passion?

Engage your imagination and do that!

Thoughts

Cluster Feed

1 Thessalonians 5:17 *"Pray without ceasing."*

You are probably wondering what kind of connection I am going to find with three words "pray without ceasing" and how I intend to relate that to motherhood.

I believe that raising children is an assignment from God and you should pray for your children without ceasing. The main connection, however minor, is that I couldn't help but notice that whenever my son is in an unfamiliar environment or needs to be soothed, he opts to be nursed. Likewise, as Christians, we should feed on the Word of God as we journey through that uncomfortable stage of our life.

When my son was 6 weeks old, we spent the afternoon with my friends Ellen, Sonia and Veronica. We talked, laughed, shared stories and then my friend commented:

- *"Ro, you nursed him like three times in the last two hours. I didn't know you cluster feed as well."*
- *What's cluster feeding?*
- *This is when a baby wants to be breastfed several times in a short period of time. It is not always due to hunger, so maybe it's because he is in a new environment with so many new faces."*

Cluster feeding, this repetitive baby initiated feeding in a short period of time is thought by experts to happen during growth spurts, or a desire for comfort when in pain, distress or in an uncomfortable or unfamiliar environment. For mothers who cluster feed, it feels like you are nursing without ceasing!

While this is a personal choice whether you feed on demand or on schedule, the Bible recommends that we pray without ceasing. Of course this does not mean that we pray for 24 hours during the day. It does, however, refer to a mindset and an attitude of prayer. You do not have to be concerned about your disposition; whether you are standing; kneeling or your eyes are closed. Praying is an important part of our relationship with God. We all know that communication is an important element in any relationship. Why would we think it would be any less important to communicate with Him?

Prayer is two-way communication with God. It is not a time to fellowship with our problems by rehearsing them. While there are different types of prayers, including one of petition, our prayer time should not be a time dedicated to laying down a list of our requests. Rather, it should be an authentic time of fellowship with your Creator. Maybe we should take the example of babies who cluster feed in unknown circumstances and feed on the Word when we don't know what to do!

Thoughts

2 ozs

As a new mother, you may spend a lot of time measuring the ounces in your little one's bottle and it is important to stop the measurements there. Please do not measure yourself or your worth to the situations of others or make comparisons.

There are enough comparisons everywhere. If you pass by a media stand, you will see magazines parading a bigger home, better body, more fashionable outfit and so much more. While it is easy to blame the media for all of our insecurities, we have to take accountability for our actions and feelings by reassuring ourselves of our worth.

I was in the waiting room of my newborn's pediatrician and engaged in a conversation with another mother who told me that her baby would not latch on to breastfeed.

In order to feed her baby, she had to pump breast milk and each time she would get a minimum of 4 ounces *per* breast in a few minutes. What? 8 ounces? I sometimes pump for twenty minutes and express 2 ounces! It was humiliating at times to talk to women who had a healthy flow or oversupply of milk. I thought back to the very few drops I would get after what felt like an eternity of pumping and resisted the temptation to feel inferior or overwhelmed.

I fought the temptation to measure, compare or weigh my worth against hers. Her success was not my failure. For this reason, I was happy to be the first out of many of my friends to experience motherhood so that I could offer guidance. I did not want them to have some of the discouraging experiences I encountered.

One day, I told my friend Camille that my ten month old baby was running around. She jokingly asked me *"Is he a genius?"* She continued *"When are babies supposed to start crawling?"* I could tell that she was starting to compare her three month old to make sure that he was on par so I responded, *"Connor James will start crawling when he is ready to start crawling"*.

My intention was not to be sarcastic or dismissive but to encourage her so that she would not fall into the trap of comparing or measuring her child's success based on others.

While statistical information can be helpful to judge whether there is a disability or medical issue, if your baby is healthy, you should not worry unnecessarily.

*Well how many pounds **should** he be at his age?*
*How many ounces **should** she be drinking?*
*When **should** he start walking?*
*When **should** she start talking?*

I've mentioned on a number of occasions that I did not express as much milk as I would have liked. What I failed to mention is that I was not pumping the recommended amount of times daily. It is recommended that you pump and nurse 8-12 times per day which equates to 2-3 hours daily. I was pumping twice per day and nursing 2-3 times per day.

It's typical to see someone else's glory but not know their story. How many times do we expect the results other people receive but are not willing to do what they did? We see the blessings but we don't see how much time they spend with God, stay on their face and knees in prayer while living a life of thanksgiving.

I beg of you, stop comparing yourselves to others and stop comparing your child with wrong motives. God has designed us so intricately that even our fingerprints are different from someone else's!

One major lesson I have learned through motherhood is the uniqueness of our bodies, preferences, and personalities. Our babies are different from others and while we may share some experiences, we may have some very different ones. On a deeper level, we must understand that when we compare, we belittle what God has done for us.

We all have our individual purpose so do not belittle what God has given you by comparing it to others or trying to be like someone else. They are doing a good job at being them and the world does not need two of them.

Be uniquely you…

Thoughts

"Because I Said So"

When we become parents, we sometimes pull rank as the final authority and opt not to explain our positions or reasons for making certain decisions.

"Mommy why do I have to do that?"
"Because I said so"

We tell our children that what we say should suffice and they shouldn't question our rationale. But do we use the same logic when our Heavenly Father graciously provides us with instructions from His infinite wisdom?

If God tells us to do something, do we need to know why? Do we need to know the full plan before we act on it? The *"Because I said so"* line never made sense to me until I became a mother and knew that my motive was pure. Proverbs 3:5 reassures us to trust in the Lord and not lean on our own understanding. Rather we should acknowledge God in all our decisions and He will direct our paths.

Who is your final authority?
What is your final authority?
Where do you go for answers?

I remember opening my son's diaper and thinking "*Oh my Lord, what are all these things in my son's diapers?*" I saw what resembled sugar crystals. I felt the texture and it had a soft jelly like feeling. Now, I have changed a number of diapers including those of my seven nieces and two nephews but I have never seen anything like this before!

Two thoughts came to mind:

Call mom.

Check the internet.

I described what I saw and I encountered a plethora of websites as many mothers experienced the same thing. While I would like to gloat that my baby is so sweet that he pees out sugar crystals; that certainly was not the case! I typically change his diaper very frequently but on this day my newborn slept for much longer than usual and his diaper was saturated.

My mother and the internet informed me that the absorbent gelling material found in diapers designed to absorb the wetness leaks out if the diaper is very wet and fitted and creates a jelly like substance. It was useful to contact the internet and definitely good to call Mama. Of course calling mom and checking the internet yields great results and is a practical source for wisdom.

But where do we go for spiritual issues? Do we quickly run to the Word of God or is the internet our final authority? Do we ask Jesus what He has to say or do we call a friend?

When I was considering my relocation to China, I told my parents and a few of my close friends about the possibility of moving to Asia and waited for their reaction. It was as if I was tallying the responses and counting ballots to come to a decision.

While it would be nice to have their blessings, I should not look to people for approval. We are inundated with opinions from media, traditions, people's philosophy and religious doctrines. We have to make a conscious effort to go to the Word of God concerning everything.

Give God that place in your life, ask Him what He thinks about what you are experiencing and submit your plans to Him. Allow Him to lead and guide you.

Who have you crowned God in your life? Don't feel condemned if you haven't made God priority, make the adjustment and make the Word of God your final authority and be persuaded that things will go as promised b*ecause **He** said so*!

Thoughts

Childproof

As parents, we nurture, teach and chastise our children because we love them. When they want something that is not beneficial to them, we refuse to satisfy their desire because we want to protect them. We childproof the house because we don't want our babies to hurt themselves. We know the reason we are doing it but the child may not understand so it may seem like we are taking away things that bring them joy.

Could it be that sometimes God removes things out of our path to protect us and not to frustrate us?

We childproof our homes to prepare for our little babies. We close doors, put up little gates, cover outlets, secure drawers, and put scratch mittens on their fingers to prevent them from cutting themselves. When my son started cruising, he muscled up enough energy to get close to a glass vase on the table but I snatched it away from him before he could get a good grasp of it. I know that may have been frustrating for him but I did not want him to hurt himself or break the vase. Could it be the same way God is ensuring our own safety, from *ourselves*?

As parents, we know that what we are doing is best, but it often frustrates our children because they don't understand what we are doing or why we are doing it.

They want to be free but we cover their hands. They want to walk through the door to see what is on the other side but we close it securely. They go after something and we take it away.

I've experienced what I like to call the three scary "F's" – **failure, frustration and fear**. To be honest, I am tremendously content with my life; however there was just one aspect that seemed to be a **failure** – my career.

I felt as if it excelled so gracefully, plummeted then plateaued. I went through a period where there was nothing that I wanted more than to leave my current job. On paper, it was a great gig! My hours were stable; I was well-compensated for my role; my managers and coworkers liked and respected me; the commute was great and the location was even better. But I did not feel a sense of purpose, I did not have impact, and the role was not fulfilling.

I applied for another job and got rejected in the same week! Recruiters flooded my email with jobs that they thought would be great for me, I would reply and then they wouldn't. Some recruiters would call me back; go through the screening and tell me how perfect I was for the role but I wouldn't get the position. Four different recruiters contacted me about the same role and I still was not chosen!

Door after door closed.

Then I moved into **frustration** and said to God, *"God I am following the formula"*. I prayed…I made confessions…I quoted scriptures… But I did not get any job leads – just silence…

There was one position that I interviewed for and I was eager to hear from them because I received positive feedback after the interview. One of the three interviewers told me that she would have liked to hire me on the spot because she was so pleased with how graceful and poised I was!

I remember being so frustrated one day because I wanted a change or at least an update about the interview. I received an email from the hiring manager stating that she was informed the day before that there was a hiring freeze because of the budget. She did not know how long the freeze would last; but she knew she could not go forward with hiring me. I was devastated. Then there was **fear**.

What if I become so stagnant in my career that I am no longer marketable or attractive to companies? What if no doors open and I get stuck in this rut of unhappiness and this unfulfilled feeling?

Could it be that God is working on the three P's?

Protection
Patience
Perseverance

God, are you protecting me from me? From making rash decisions because I am bored? Emotional decisions because I am fed up; illogical ones because I am tired of the routine? Are you keeping me in a stable job because you foresee something I can't? Or am I dreaming too small and you want to give me something greater?

Perspective is very important because often times what we consider rejection is actually protection. Remember that person who broke your heart or mistreated you? Imagine if you married that joker! Thank God that relationship didn't work out! How about the job that you didn't receive? You were frustrated and felt like all the doors were shut, but hindsight is 20/20 and I am sure you can look back and realize that either there was a better role for you; the one that you wanted would have negatively affected your quality of life; or maybe it was time to start your entrepreneurial endeavors.

I regained my peace knowing that as long as I have Christ in me, failure is not an option and that God loves me and His plans for me are good! Our Heavenly Father knows the plans He has for us and they are not to harm us but rather to give us a great future.

So the next time you don't get what you want, ask God if He is protecting you from yourself; from your rash decisions or limited vision.

Thoughts

Baby Steps

I learned a lot about trust and faith by watching my son on a daily basis. He trusted that I would not allow him to fall, even when I threw him up in the air. He is never anxious about the provision of his needs; wondering where his food, clothes, or diapers would come from. I decided that I would adopt the calm disposition knowing that my steps are ordered and learn to take baby steps in areas of my life that are new territory and continue to take leaps of faith as I maneuvered through life on my walk with God.

I searched through the Bible for the word *"walk"* and three scriptures stood out to me to teach me how to walk.

Walk in the Spirit

Galatians 5:25 "If we live in the Spirit, let us also walk in the Spirit."

What does it mean to walk in the Spirit? How do you know that you are walking in the Spirit? It will sound pretty spooky if you do not have a true understanding of the content.

One of the best ways to tell a type of tree is by the fruit it bears, right? So what are the fruits of walking in the Spirit?

The Fruits of the Spirit are *love, joy, peace, patience, kindness, goodness, faithfulness, gentleness and self-control.* A demonstration of these fruits is an indication that you are walking in the Spirit. It means relying on God to empower you through His grace to produce the fruits of the Spirit. Grace is an empowerment that allows us to walk in the Spirit so that we will not fulfill the undesirable yearnings of our physical senses.

Walk by faith

2 Corinthians 5:7 "For we walk by faith, not by sight."

We should not be moved by what we see, hear or feel. Do not place trust in your physical senses or struggle to believe. Do not be distracted by what you see or don't see. More importantly, do not be moved by how you feel. Emotions will move you in various directions but when you walk by faith, you will have a favorable destination.

My steps are ordered by God

Psalm 37:23 *"The steps of a good man are ordered by the Lord: and He delights in his way."*

Every time a baby takes a step, they are displaying an act of faith. They do not have a guarantee or assurance that the next step will not result in a fall or wobbling to the floor, but they muster up the courage to take that step.

Take baby steps until you develop and mature in the Word of God and are able to walk in the Spirit by faith. It is more important to take a step than to be crippled in the limbo of fear and indecision.

Finally, trust that your steps are ordered by God and that He is leading and guiding you.

Make God your GPS (God Positioning System)!

Thoughts

Learning To Talk (Imitating Christ)

"When I was a child, I felt as a child, I thought as a child, now that I am become a man, I have to put away childish things."
1 Corinthians 13:11

I have a friend who was born in the Democratic Republic of Congo, lived in France and now lives in South Africa. Her name is Linda and she speaks French beautifully. I was so impressed by her ability to speak French that I asked her to help me with my pronunciation.

The first phrase I wanted to learn was, *"Je voudrais trouver l'amour,"* which hails from the popular French song *"Je m'appelle Hélène"*. The English translation is "I would like to find love". Linda said the word "je voudrais" and asked me to repeat it so I did. She then repeated it slower and I copied her tone and inflection and confidently delivered the phrase.

Clearly she was not satisfied with my rendition of the words and said it even more phonetically than the first two times. I watched the way she moved her lips and I was impressed by how identical I *thought* I repeated it.

I smiled very pleased with myself, and then she smiled and said assuredly *"It will come."* I protested, *"What do you mean it will come? It came!"* We both burst into laughter.

Similar to my encounter with French, when my son was four months, he babbled long sentences with such confidence in what he was saying. He watched my mouth closely, listened to my words, and then tried to imitate me. He was learning how to talk and trying to align his words with mine. As he matures, he will stop babbling and start speaking words that can be understood.

As believers, we should align our speech with the words of our Heavenly Father. We must speak with boldness the way Jesus spoke to the devil when He was being tempted. We must confidently declare our identity the way Jesus told His persecutors that He is the Son of God. Jesus spoke to see what He spoke.

The world was formed by the power of words so if we are going to speak, we need to know how to speak and what to speak. A king makes declarations to enable manifestations. We need to balance doing and spend more time declaring. It is important to make a conscious decision about the words we speak because they are powerful and have transforming power. Grace will teach you how to speak and empower you to speak life into every circumstance.

"Be imitators of Christ." Ephesians 5:1

Thoughts

About the Author

Thank you for reading this book, I hope you enjoyed *7 lbs 13 ozs* and you feel inspired to live your best life. I know that there were some radical truths in this book but I truly believe that God wants His best for you and that being plagued with stress, worry, pain and anxiety is absolutely not God's best!

I challenge you to reject the societal norms, use your life to dispel myths and experience a supernatural life. I pray that you enjoy the journey of motherhood and your relationship with God. I believe that life is filled with choices and it is a series of decisions. You can live your life by your fears or by His promises and I pray that you choose to live by His promises!

Being a *mompreneur* is a new journey because I never desired to be a business woman. I wanted my 9-5 job with my four weeks of vacation time so I could travel, return to a stable job, go home to my family and do it all over again.

Then I realized that there is a greater reason for my existence than sitting behind a desk meeting someone else's bottom-line. I believe my experiences, journey and lessons learned should be documented so others can benefit and be empowered. So I started writing…

I also believe that women are precious jewels so I inspire women to know their worth and never compromise their values. I challenge women by asking questions designed for introspection to ignite a desire to take an internal course of action. Out of this vision, Rose-Anne Uwague's Beauty Evolution **(RUBE)** was birthed to dispel unrealistic standards of beauty and encourage women to embrace their unique identity. RUBE (pronounced ruby) is a cosmetic brand that started with lipsticks fused with empowering reminders that outer beauty can be enhanced and inner beauty should be cultivated.

My heart aches for children who do not have access to basic human rights which I consider to be water, food and education. Out of this burning desire to make a change, **Rare** was born.

My Story

Prior to becoming Mrs. Rose-Anne Uwague, I was Rose-Anne Angus. I am an American born Jamaican who lived in Jamaica until I was 16 years old.

I moved to New York to start college. I graduated with an Associate in Applied Sciences in Travel, Tourism and Hospitality; a Bachelor of Arts and Master of Arts in Business Communications by the age of 21.

A few months after graduating, I moved to China as a foreign expert to teach English and I lived there for two years. I had an amazing experience and then returned to New York. I speak Mandarin Chinese, speak some Spanish and butcher French.

I am still a professional in the corporate world and I take passion in speaking engagements discussing RUBE, motherhood and female empowerment.

Christ is the central element of my life. I am the wife of Izoduwa Uwague and mommy to our son Hadar (a Hebrew word for beauty, power and splendor of God).

I am an avid globetrotter and a lover of food and culture. I love to laugh, eat and enjoy new adventures.

Connect with the Author

Send your feedback, comments, thoughts or questions!

Email: 7lbs13ozs@gmail.com

Website: www.roseanneuwague.com

Instagram: @ruwague

Twitter: @rouwague

www.ingramcontent.com/pod-product-compliance
Lightning Source LLC
Chambersburg PA
CBHW070204100426
42743CB00013B/3046